CONCENTRATION

Arne Weingart

FUTURECYCLE PRESS
www.futurecycle.org

Cover artwork, "Concentration camp uniform jacket with badge worn by a Lithuanian Jewish inmate" (from the United States Holocaust Memorial Museum Collection, Gift of George J. Fine); cover and interior book design by Diane Kistner; author photo by Karen Weingart; ITC New Baskerville text and titling

Library of Congress Control Number: 2022946009

Copyright © 2023 Arne Weingart
All Rights Reserved

Published by FutureCycle Press
Athens, Georgia, USA

ISBN 978-1-952593-45-1

To the disappeareds

We must embrace our existence to the fullest extent; everything, including what is most unthinkable, must be possible within it. This is essentially the only bravery that can be demanded of us; to show courage in the face of the strangest, most grotesque and inexplicable events that we could possibly experience.

—Rainer Maria Rilke
from *Letters to a Young Poet*

PROLOGUE

I try to think what happened in cafés
when we were in cafés. Or sitting in
the park when there were parks. When there was time
for staring through a thick tobacco haze
at nothing. Waiting for something to begin
we somehow had agreed would be sublime.
I can't remember what it was we thought.
Only that there was music in the air
of the most modern type. The love we sought
was temporary but profound. If there
were verses we expected them to rhyme.

I.

Upon a background of navy and off-white
three-centimeter stripes we know each other.
Yellow underlying triangle badges
for Jews. Then overlaying inverted
triangles. Red for the politicals.
Green for the criminals. Forced laborers
get blue. Then purple for Jehovah's Witnesses.
Male homosexuals are pink. Slackers
get black and Gypsies brown. There are initials
for nationalities and bars and circles
for repeaters race traitors and escapers.

II.

What is my job here? To keep myself alive?
For example: If I die am I no longer working?
Or is that also my job? To die. At the right time.
For example: When a train comes in and
the selection is made and they tell me
to lead a group to the right and their barracks
I go right. And if they tell me to lead a group
to the left and the showers I go left. I go
where they tell me. Are these then my wages?
For example: If I were to ask for a raise would that
mean what I wanted was a little more life?

III.

Last things first. You can't imagine
what it's like in a world without porcelain
can you? I can't and it's the only world
I know now. Not the eating kind.
Or the sitting on a bookshelf kind.
Never mind there are no bookshelves.
No books. I mean the kind for sitting on
and shitting in. The cold smooth white stone
that resists all indignity and is connected
to endless water. No matter what they
feed you it doesn't mean that you don't shit.

IV.

I heard this rumor. My friend swears it's true.
But my friend is dead. There was a couple.
I can't think they met here. But there was
a couple. And they wanted to get pregnant.
So the groom ejaculated onto a piece of string.
What else could he find that wouldn't be
noticed by the guards? And he passed it on
to someone who could pass it through
the electrified fence to someone who could
pass it on to the bride. I want to be that child.
Born where nothing can possibly get worse.

V.

It's true I have forsaken the old god.
The one I could never pray to without
seeing myself praying and seeing someone
who looked like a fool. And I'm not a fool.
It's not so much that I lacked faith but that
I never wanted faith to interfere
with thinking. Now I think the Nazi gods
are fierce and terrifying and efficient
but ultimately too competitive for
their own good. Kind of like the Greek
gods were. We'll see. And as for Jesus. Please.

VI.

Cold. Have you ever gone out for the paper
in your pajamas? Perhaps also a robe
and slippers while it starts to snow those tight
dry flakes you know will still be on the ground
at the end of the worst week of the worst
winter you can remember. Now look at
your door. Half open. Waiting for you.
A door you will never again walk through.
This is a different winter. But the cold
is the same cold. And you are standing in it
in your pajamas while the roll is called.

VII.

What's the word for when the wind is right
and you can't suddenly decide to stop
breathing? Can't avoid the smoke and the light
white ash that covers everything always.
We're not cannibals. Not yet. But the stomach
was made to forgive and forget everything.
Not so the lungs. We breathe each other in.
We are the fuel for this strange factory.
We are the air and the mud and the wheel.
We are cause and effect and everything between.
Forgiveness and remembrance can wait.

VIII.

Was I in love once? I was of an age
to be in love. It almost happened once
or twice. It happens when it happens
I told myself. Sooner better than later.
Later better than never. I never thought
now or never. Then never became now.
The barely shaving soldiers who corralled us
in the streets must have been in love. Some of them.
With Trudi or Heidi or Hildi or Leni.
Love will not save them. It will not save me.
I don't want saving. I just want to live.

IX.

We were asleep my dead friend liked to say.
My other friends are also dead but they
still hold their bowls out for the soup which is
not soup exactly. Not precisely. Not at all.
We were asleep but free. Now we're awake
in chains. I don't know what the others dream
but I have yet to wake up frightened. Nothing
scares me more than when my eyes are open.
There's bound to be a market I would wager
for dreams that make it out of here alive.
You'll have to hold that bet. Or give me credit.

X.

Remember the last time you were naked?
No one here does because to be unclothed
and standing barefoot in orderly rows
can only mean that soon you will be heading
skeptically for the showers. You could use
a shower now after that long train ride.
There are no showers here. I think some part of you
already knows this. Perhaps the naked part
which has never been fooled before. It knows
what it knows and cannot be lied to. But here
there are no naked people. Not anymore.

XI.

I have a number on my arm. Six digits.
I am apparently being kept count of
for reasons I do not yet understand.
As much as I would like an explanation
no one is volunteering one and I
know better than to ask. What we all know.
We in the camp. Is that a German. Any German.
Feels better looking at a row of numbers
than at a blank page in the ledger book.
Is this a weakness or a strength? At least
I know I'm worth the ink in my tattoo.

XII.

Why do they hate us? Can it be because
they do not sufficiently love themselves?
OK. Maybe. But that seems a little simple
even for the current circumstances
which strongly suggest that the simple answer
is the best answer. What is it that we did
or failed to do? And keep on doing or
not doing? I give up. You tell me. Please.
We have been playing tag for centuries
and we are always it. Why are the others
allowed to run and hide? I'll count to ten.

XIII.

You'd think cause and effect might have agreed
to stay married to each other. But cause
has moved out and is living with his mistress.
Effect has filed her papers for divorce.
The kids have all been sent to camp. We are
not doing particularly well. There is
the food for one thing. At least no one makes us
write home. We are however getting our
fair share of exercise. We are not the same
indolent children. And as for arts and crafts
I only hope they don't outlive their learning.

XIV.

So what if we killed Christ? I'm not admitting
we did. But just suppose we didn't do
everything that we might have managed to
keep him alive. We weren't the rulers of
Jerusalem any more than we governed Rome.
Who would have felt maximally threatened by
one scraggly charismatic footloose Jew?
Not us. And by us I of course mean them.
Those priests and hangers-on who even then
could feel their time was past. Who even then
could not agree on anything. Like us.

XV.

Lampshades and bars of soap. This is a myth
you might be thinking. I am here to tell you
that it is not. The photographs don't lie.
I know because I took them. It's my job.
Along with hauling bodies from the showers
which are not showers. Before the war
I liked to go out with my camera.
A Leica naturally. I thought I might
do something with it on the borderline
of art. If there were borders I have crossed them.
You can't imagine what I do for bread.

XVI.

I'd kill you for a cigarette. That's what
my friend said just before they put a shovel
in his hands and made him dig a trench
along with a few dozen other shovelers.
Not very deep because the light was almost
disappearing and the ground was hard.
So hard. Then all at once they grabbed
the shovels back and pushed them in the pit
and started shooting indiscriminately.
By which I mean they couldn't be bothered
to aim. Friend I could also use a smoke.

XVII.

And you. Who are you and where might you be?
What makes me think you even exist? Your
silence is its own perfect animal.
Like the stuffed giraffe from childhood I held on to
long past its magic powers to ward off
the evil I was terrified might find me.
It turns out I was right about the evil
but wrong that it was interested in me
in particular. Evil doesn't make
such fine distinctions. But it still depends
on silence. If you're reading this you know.

XVIII.

What do you do with ten thousand gold fillings?
Melt them down into ten gold bullion bricks
with which to buy ten aeroplane propellers?
Or endless leather and cardboard suitcases
full of what can be snatched from an entire life
in ten minutes? Someone must have thought
of all this in advance don't you imagine?
Someone not exactly at the top
or at the bottom of this great machine.
But someone in the middle with a wrench
and an oil can. Wearing a uniform.

XIX.

I haven't seen a lot of suicides.
I mean I haven't seen any unless
you count a stumble into the barbed wire fence
with current running through it. But who's counting?
My theory is it's too hard to keep living
and the effort is what's keeping us alive
or maybe just distracted. Some of us
die like Shakespeare's flies. Worn out. At random.
But others of us are more like the insect
described at length by Kafka. Self-aware
and disconcerted. Driven by complaint.

XX.

A sense of time. I think I had one once.
More like an expectation of events
that happen in a certain order. But when
death is never not the next thing that
could happen time begins to bend or float
or fade or disconnect. All days the one day.
All hours the one hour. Every night
the single night which might be the last night.
You see the problem. My friend had a watch
he traded for some moldy bread. I still
can see him staring at his naked wrist.

XXI.

I might be seeing things. They smashed my glasses
the minute I stepped off the train. You'd think
I'd be a better laborer if only
I could see what I was supposed to be doing.
There must be Nazi regulations that
insist on introducing the idea
of chaos early on. But I found others.
Glasses I mean. Spectacles have a way
of outliving their former wearers here.
Seeing is believing. And we see
plenty. My stolen sight will outlive me.

XXII.

Why don't they bomb the camps? All of them.
Or at least some of them. Or just this one.
Or me. Just bomb the Jesus out of me.
Am I too insignificant a target?
I'd settle for collateral damage
and the chance to run. Where to it doesn't matter.
There's nothing to run back to if you want
my unasked for opinion. Back is not
an option. Back is what delivered us here
and killed us. Forward is a lie a joke
a dream and an illusion. Bomb us now.

XXIII.

The women went on strike. Not so the men.
The women thought that on account of how
their female guards were more approachable.
More likely to return a smile or toss
an extra heel of bread around or the
occasional potato they might make
a demonstration on behalf of some
reasonable proposition I forget which.
At dawn they called a dozen women out
at roll call. Lined them up and shot them.
Same thing at evening roll call. The men wept.

XXIV.

So how do you translate ARBEIT MACHT FREI?
It's not as though we don't know what it means.
We speak the language. Most of us. We know
what the intention of the letters is.
I hate to say it now but once I loved
the Germans for their irony. No one
could be as amusing or as amused
by their own wit. But I don't think we are
presently being tortured by an army
of ironists. Sincerity can kill you
but no one ever died of irony.

XXV.

We have a band you know. Some of us play
or rather played an instrument when music
was as natural and unpretentious as
breathing. Now we count our breaths like measures
which I suppose was the original
idea. We rehearse in the short interval
between supper which is not supper
and sleep which is not sleep. We play what we
can still remember without looking at
a score. Sheet music is as scarce
as the light from incarcerated stars.

XXVI.

I'm glad to say we finally have an answer
to precisely who is and who is not
a Jew. If you were on the train then Jew.
If you die quietly here then more a Jew.
If you resist somehow then perhaps less
a Jew and more a human being. If
you neither fight nor die you are the most
Jewish it is possible to be.
And the most human. If you live and are
asked how you stayed alive what will you say?
That it was all some sort of big mistake?

XXVII.

I miss my parents. Even though I tried
to stay as far away from them as possible
while I was making up my mind about what
I might become. What does it matter now?
They have become the fire and the ash
that follows fire and the ghosts that follow ashes.
And I have become a tree in a thinning forest
dodging the swing of a clumsy axe.
Also I miss my sister. I never found out
where they might have taken her. Or even if
she still exists. You. Yes you. Please find her.

XXVIII.

Somehow we all ended up living in
our own museums. Mine was The Museum
Of Culture And Detachment. Not a place
likely to survive the first bombardment.
Others took shelter behind the walls
of Piety And Faith And Ignorance
In Spite Of Everything which as an institution
is unimpregnable in normal circumstances.
But most are currently waiting out the war
in The Museum Of Railroads That Run
On Time No Matter Where They Might Be Going.

XXIX.

In the future. Not mine. I mean your future.
Someone will likely say it is barbaric
to use poetic form to talk about
what happens when the world is at its worst.
It's not an argument that holds up well.
What Homer saw was not a life less horrible.
We know antiquity was not polite.
Somehow the oldest Greek and Roman statues
still look a lot like us. And when I stare
at Venus cold and armless where she poses
my blood still rises. How do you explain that?

XXX.

We who are dirty would like to be clean
again. But there's a problem when the men
the elders of the tribe whose matted beards
smell of egg yellow garlic and spilled tea
decide what makes a woman pure and when.
For now the men can no longer decide.
The women being practical don't care.
Our jailors and exterminators think
we are the problem. Also the solution.
But only if we disappear. I want
to stand in a hot shower for a year.

XXXI.

You'd think that birds would be forbidden here.
That somehow they would know not to appear
as usual and sing and fight and fly
and squat on branches. Balance on barbed wire.
Look down on us with a kind of cruel
immunity. Especially the crows
who seem particularly unsurprised.
Something must have seen all of this before
and learned to act as though nothing were wrong.
The crow comes with his prehistoric news.
Each morning I awake to hear his song.

XXXII.

We never believed in science. Not really.
Or in religion although you might think
if anything required believing it was
belief itself. But ask God. If you still believe
in God. And let me know what God replies.
They were convenient. Science and religion.
They helped us fall asleep. They were a reason
to wake up. But none of that matters now.
The new god doesn't care what you believe in.
The new religion is not God but blood.
And blood believes in nothing. Not even us.

XXXIII.

My dead friend never got to hear his eulogy.
Not in the place where the words might best have
fallen on his unhearing ears. The coffin
safe in a grave in some neglected cemetery
close to home. Instead a hidden shallow ditch
in a snow-covered fallow Polish field.
I would have said: I didn't know you well.
But all the same I knew enough. You were
not weak and not afraid. You understood
that what is normally impossible
is not impossible. You made me laugh.

XXXIV.

Who can trust history again? We trust each other
now less than a feral cat trusts the hand
that feeds it. We look each other in the eye
only to challenge or surrender. We are
being bred back to savagery. Those of us
who manage to survive. How will we
open a book again and believe the ink?
Allow the paper to carry us forward
on a sea of words which are not ours?
I would rather you read the numbers on my arm.
Count out my vertebrae with your living fingers.

XXXV.

I am not ill if you compare me to
others who are so far from well
a day or two at most separates them
from the cost of a bullet and the ride
on a full cart to the incinerator.
Work or die. I work and die a little
every day. And some hang on like climbers
abandoned high up on the mountain
who can neither go up nor go down
again. Who seem to like it where the air
is thin. Where walking is the most like flying.

XXXVI.

Sometimes there is a moment in the night
after the last cough in an enormous room
full of coughing when it is possible
to think of the existence of a different
physics. Not less deterministic
or indifferent. But one where the rules
allow for light to occasionally bend
in unpredictable directions. Where gravity
masquerades as levity. And where time
is less dependent on our knowing when.
This gives me hope. Then someone coughs again.

XXXVII.

In my family before me and my sister.
Generations back. Everyone worked in
one of the needle trades. Tailor. Glovemaker.
Furrier. Milliner. They would not have
imagined themselves artists or designers.
Rather craftsmen in an ancient guild.
Old photos show them dressed up like royalty
out for a walk among the common folk.
Such stern self-satisfaction. It was a joke
they all were in on. Lucky for me
in spite of everything I don't mind stripes.

XXXVIII.

Marx never thought this kind of factory
could possibly exist. But Marx was wrong.
Labor may be a fixed commodity
in normal work. Normal does not belong
here strictly. Here labor expires by plan.
When there are no more laborers the work
is ipso facto finished. The last man
is the last actual product. Shadows lurk
in the abandoned factory. Quelle mistake!
Marx tries to think back to where he began.
Why would you feed a self-devouring snake?

XXXIX.

I have a pocket. Not everyone does.
My dead friend had none which is how I came
to be in possession of two small packs
of French cigarette papers. Qualité
Supérieure. Zig Zag. Thirty-two leaves
apiece or what was left. Nothing resembling
tobacco. No matches. In such a manner
my friend's bequest became my writing journal.
Pencils were harder but the girls who sift
the clothing prior to the gas for valuables
help out. How many die so I can write?

XL.

I can't help thinking what would Rilke think
who taught us how to see hope and affliction
and beauty and love and hopelessness
with the same admiring tightly focused eye.
It was exhilarating reading him
and feeling at once ancient and the most
modern it might be possible to be.
I'm not the same reader. Despite the power
I might have felt in that unchanging place
the world that changed me is not Rilke's world.
If he were here he wouldn't last an hour.

XLI.

What kind of girl would want me for a lover
should I survive? I think only someone
who had been here. Who saw with her own eyes
what no one should have ever seen. Otherwise
I'd be like some explorer who returns
from his great journey only to retreat
into a life of silence. We would each need
someone to say nothing to forever
and not feel guilty or beside desire.
Someone who saw you walk out of the fire
and pretends not to mind the smell of smoke.

XLII.

Something has changed. The trains come in less often.
Mainly from other camps. Grief upon grief
but in a slightly different uniform.
Different tailors. Different fabric.
Different thread. But the same gray faces
as our faces. By now we all are sharing
the same face of which there is only one
between us. We all thought we were all
different. Everyone does. Everyone did.
We might have learned to live inside this place
but not without a cost. I hate my face.

XLIII.

Geraniums in window boxes. Once
they marched us past the officers' barracks
for no apparent reason on the way
to work. Boredom I think. Or schadenfreude
which you could bottle here like mother's milk.
In our part of Silesia the spring
can wound you worse than winter. Red and green
assaulted us. Opened for us a window
into lost life even as we were losing it.
Give us back our filthy grays and browns.
Our ashy shadows. Give us back our black.

XLIV.

When they find us if they find us we will be
almost impossible to look at. We are
occupants of a planet whose existence
is theoretically conceded but
upon which no human wishes to tread.
We are both sub- and superhuman. Therefore
alien and never to be trusted.
We will grow back our human flesh and hair.
Regain our appetites. Our base desires.
But looking at us you will feel a judgement
descend. May you be judged. But not by us.

XLV.

They've started piling corpses up against
a wall. This is not normal based on all
that passes for normal. Regardless we
are not alarmed. We've seen how the supply
of bodies can so easily exceed
demand inside our little factory.
Things even out. Death. Life. The natural need
for order inside chaos. Eventually
a plan will be revealed only to be
cancelled or forgotten. But meanwhile they
are piling corpses up against a wall.

XLVI.

I can't tell every story. Even if
I wanted to. And I don't want to.
I won't be responsible for your knowing
or not knowing. If you want to know
come here when it is safe to come and place
your hands on whatever is still standing.
Take off your shoes and socks and feel the dirt
which stays mysteriously cold. Go out
beyond the gate into the field and put
your ear up to the grass. If you hear something.
Good. If you hear nothing. Even better.

XLVII.

I always thought I'd be the last to leave.
I was prepared to be dead or be here
until the end. Whatever the end meant.
But now I'm marching east. Assuming east
is still a place that can be gotten to.
And we're not marching really. Only falling
forward. It is spring and it is cold
and there is snow and there are few enough
of us that the guards who must also march
can no longer pretend not to know us.
I may be wrong but the war may be over.

XLVIII.

You'll probably want to know if I'm alive.
That's if you still believe in narrative.
One thing followed by yet another thing
and so on. The gun resting on the mantle
in the first act that goes off in the third.
Or doesn't. You can't help wanting to feel
you know something about the world. I can't
help it either and I know less than nothing.
But I was not trapped in a fairytale.
There were no kings. No spells. No princesses.
In the deep wood no monsters. Only men.

EPILOGUE

A march is not a walk. I never knew
the difference not having marched before.
A march is what you can be made to do.
Walk. Run. Skip. Saunter. But you march to war.
You march to battle. Walk back in retreat
or run the way you've never run before.
It has to do with how you point your feet.
Although you march to battle run from war.
Take my word as a coward at the front.
I'm tired of marching where they tell me to.
A march is what you can be made to do.

About FutureCycle Press

FutureCycle Press is dedicated to publishing lasting English-language poetry in both print-on-demand and Kindle formats. Founded in 2007 by long-time independent editor/publishers and partners Diane Kistner and Robert S. King, the press was incorporated as a nonprofit in 2012. A number of our editors are distinguished poets and writers in their own right, and we have been actively involved in the small press movement going back to the early seventies.

Each year, we award the FutureCycle Poetry Book Prize and honorarium for the best original full-length volume of poetry we published that year. Introduced in 2013, proceeds from our Good Works projects are donated to charity. Our Selected Poems series highlights contemporary poets with a substantial body of work to their credit; with this series we strive to resurrect work that has had limited distribution and is now out of print.

We are dedicated to giving all of the authors we publish the care their work deserves, offering a catalog of the most diverse and distinguished work possible, and paying forward any earnings to fund more great books. All of our books are kept "alive" and available unless and until an author requests a title be taken out of print.

We've learned a few things about independent publishing over the years. We've also evolved a unique and resilient publishing model that allows us to focus mainly on vetting and preserving for posterity poetry collections of exceptional quality without becoming overwhelmed with bookkeeping, mailing, fundraising activities, or taxing editorial and production "bubbles." To find out more about what we are doing, come see us at futurecycle.org.

The FutureCycle Poetry Book Prize

All original, full-length poetry books published by FutureCycle Press in a given calendar year are considered for the FutureCycle Poetry Book Prize. This allows us to consider each submission on its own merits, outside of the context of a traditional contest. Too, the judges see the finished book, which will have benefitted from the beautiful book design and strong editorial gloss we are famous for.

The book ranked the best in judging is announced as the prize-winner in January of the subsequent year. There is no fixed monetary award; instead, the winning poet receives an honorarium of 20% of the total net royalties from all poetry books and chapbooks the press sold online in the year the winning book was published. The winner is also accorded the honor of being on the panel of judges for the next year's competition; judges receive copies of the contending books to keep for their personal library.